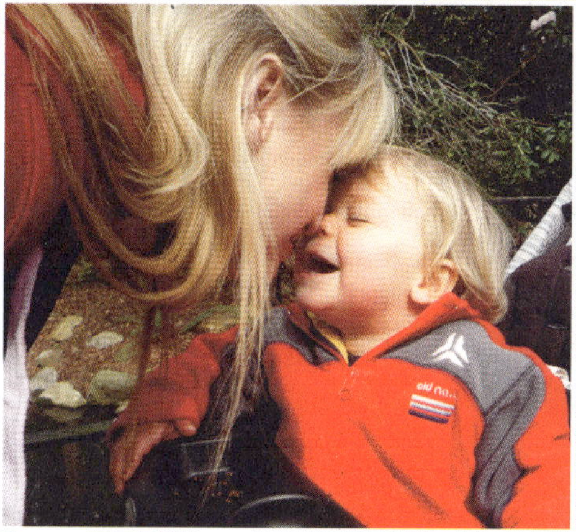

Colophon

Moments that Speak: Stories and Images of Connection

KIT Publishers bv
Mauritskade 63
P.O. Box 95001
1090 HA Amsterdam
The Netherlands
publishers@kit.nl
www.kit.nl/publishers

Editors: Lisa Marika Jokivirta, Anna Duhon, Shannon Walsh

International Advisory and Editorial Team:
Alide Roerink (Netherlands); Alicia Jimenez (Costa Rica); Barbara Lorraine Laing (Canada/UK); Betty McDermott Dobles (Costa Rica); Camila Argolo Godinho (Brazil); Dominic Stucker (USA/Germany); Douglas F. Williamson (USA); Ferdinand JC Haselaar (Netherlands); Ibrahim Al-Zu'bi (UAE); Jaana Hirsikangas (Finland); Jakub Kahul (Poland); Dumisani Nyoni (Zimbabwe); Henriette Rasmussen (Greenland); Karim El Mantawi (Egypt); Laurie Lane-Zucker (USA); Mamata Pandya (India); Mary Evelyn Tucker (USA); Mirian Vilela (Brazil); Mulenga Mulenga Cliff (Zambia); Nora Mahmoud (Tunisia/USA); Sam Crowell (USA)

Graphic design: Ad van Helmond, Amsterdam
Production: High Trade bv, Zwolle

Cover photo: Autumn in Bangladesh - three girls laugh while playing with kash flowers along the Bhrahmaputra riverbank in northern Bangladesh, photo by Fahim Hossain

isbn 978-94-6022-208-5

MIX
Paper from responsible sources
FSC® C106954
www.fsc.org

Moments that Speak is generously funded by:

Earth Charter

The Earth Charter is a declaration of fundamental ethical principles for building a just, sustainable and peaceful global society in the 21st century. It seeks to inspire in all people a new sense of global interdependence and shared responsibility for the well-being of the whole human family, the greater community of life, and future generations. It is a product of a decade-long, worldwide, cross cultural dialogue on common goals and shared values.
www.earthcharter.org

Her Majesty Queen Beatrix of the Netherlands has raised attention for the Earth Charter in the context of the urgent need for sustainable development: "Earth, our home, is alive with a unique community of life. The global environment with its finite resources is a common concern of all peoples. The protection of Earth's vitality, diversity, and beauty is a sacred trust."

This book was a project of the Youth Leadership Team, Earth Charter International.

The publisher and editors wish to extend their gratitude to the following individuals and organizations for making the first edition of this book possible: Earth Charter Secretariat (Costa Rica); Bisonte Foundation, KIT Publishers, NCDO (Netherlands); David Suzuki Foundation (Canada); and Greenbelt Movement (Kenya).

photo: martin rowe

This book is dedicated in memory of
Wangari Maathai (1940-2011)

*"It's the little things citizens do.
That's what will make the difference.
My little thing is planting trees."*

Table of Contents

A trio of children in Mukdahan, Thailand explore the shallow waters near their home.
photo by azli jamil

Acknowledgements

Looking back on our three-year journey, we are deeply humbled by the countless individuals, moments of connection, and hours of hard work and dedication that have brought this book to life.

We would especially like to thank:

Mirian Vilela and Alide Roerink, the two unsung heroes of the book, for your generous support and participation in the project, for your unending dedication to the Earth Charter, and for your belief in the power of youth to affect positive change in this world. Thank you for being such leaders of the heart. You are an inspiration to us all.

Dominic Stucker, for sharing with us so many ideas and insights, for dedicating many hours to planning and proofreading, and for feeding our spirits with your wise and caring ways. You are an inspiring father, sustainability leader and lifelong friend.

The Earth Charter Youth Leadership Team, for your support and friendship ever since we first came together in Ahmedabad. Aparna Susarla (India), Didier Gleyzes (France), Gabi Monteiro (Brazil), Hind Ottmani (Morocco), Jana Kovandzic (Serbia), Namir Nava (Mexico), Niu Keija (China), Samer Eid (Palestine), Timothy Ogene (Nigeria), and Yuyun Harmano (Indonesia)—you are testament to the power of young people, passions, and new possibilities. Keep on moving mountains in your respective corners of the globe.

Sam Crowell and Jessica Moe, for helping plant the seeds of this project, and watering them with your enthusiasm, insights, patience, and care. You never know what might come out of a day's hike up a mountain in Ciudad Colón, or an afternoon brainstorming session under the rainfall, notebooks and umbrellas in hand. We are deeply grateful to you both.

Our International Advisory and Editorial Committee, for so generously offering your insights, ideas and feedback on the text.

The Earth Charter Team—Jaana Hirsikangas (Finland) for your above-and-beyond support and website creation, as well as ***the Earth Charter staff***—Alicia Jimenez (Costa Rica), Betty McDermott Dobles (Costa Rica), Douglas F. Williamson (USA), and Nora Mahmoud (Tunisia/USA) for supporting this project in so many ways.

Marina Bakhnova (Russia), for your kind, compassionate and graceful presence; for making us laugh with your stories, and for teaching us so much. You very much remain alive in our hearts.

The David Suzuki Foundation and Greenbelt Movement for your invaluable contributions to this book.

The Academy of Finland and ***Finnish Graduate School of Environmental Social Sciences*** for providing the time, flexibility and creative space needed to finalize this project.

Above all, the hundreds of people who contributed from all over the world—both those featured in this book, and the many others we were unable to include—for so bravely and thoughtfully sharing with us your personal stories and photos. We thank you. Your words, your stories and your images very much stay with us.

Foreword

BY MARY EVELYN TUCKER

Renewing Ourselves; Renewing Earth

There is a beauty in this world that comes upon us unexpectedly and at transitional times of day – especially at dawn when the day opens up and at dusk when the day draws back into itself. These moments of transition have been observed by humans for centuries. We gather at dawn to greet the rising sun and at twilight when the sun sinks gradually from view.

Such magical moments of transition slow us down, attuning us to the spread of pink and purple across the sky. We are placed at the axis of our turning Earth so that we imagine the sun is rising or setting. But in fact it is we who are turning!

What a curious thing this is—dawn and dusk that awaken us to our own transition in relation to the sun. For we are realizing now, as never before in human history, that we are part of a great turning community of life, on a magnificent blue-green planet swirling in immense space around a vast star, our sun, which gives off energy for all life. We are now awakening to the fact that we are part of the Journey of the Universe and members of an Earth community. Is this not something to marvel at?

That is just what this collection of essays and photographs does. Each awakens us to wonder and to celebrate our deep connection to life's myriad forms. Each contributor—like every one of us—has been deeply affected by moments of connection at some point in their lives. This connection is critical in our transition towards a sustainable future. Without such connection, to others, to the Earth, to ourselves, our future will be clearly diminished. With this connection our sense of belonging and responsibility is enlarged. Comprehensive compassion can thus emerge.

The Earth Charter invites us into this interconnected worldview: "Humanity is part of a vast evolving universe. Earth, our home, is alive with a unique community of life."

The emergence of this spectacular biodiversity is due to the magnificent unfolding of life over billions of years. This book draws us into such wonders of biodiversity as the astounding beauty of hawks and woodpeckers, the graceful leap of frogs and the slippery movement of snakes, the quiet of forests that soothe us and the force of fires that humble us. It brings us into the presence of glaciers that cool us and rain that nurtures us, the power of earthquakes and tsunamis that call us to community, and the words of a child or the click of a camera that re-center us on what matters. With images and metaphors, these essays weave us back into the story of life. In so doing they provide inspiration for the great work still ahead.

All of these stories celebrate the powers of the universe and Earth to bring forth life, and sustain it. They bring us into the heart of the Earth Charter, which is "reverence for the mystery of being, gratitude for the gift of life, and humility regarding the human place in nature". With this spirit we will indeed bring the energies of renewal to ourselves, to our Earth community, to our home.

Introduction

BY LISA MARIKA JOKIVIRTA & ANNA DUHON

This book was born out of a belief in the power of a single moment of connection to bring about transformative change.

The seeds of this project were planted over an evening of storytelling and spicy curry around a crowded dinner table in Ahmedabad, India. We had come together for the first time as a group of twelve young sustainability leaders, representing five continents and together forming the Earth Charter Youth Leadership Team. As the evening progressed, the stories we shared grew deeper and more personal—about our families, our everyday lives, and what had prompted our interest in sustainability.

Towards the end of the dinner, a quiet member of the group decided to share his own story about growing up in Palestine. He described everyday life in the Gaza Strip—the beauty of the landscape, his plans to start up his own NGO, but also the shortage of water, the armed conflict, and the constant sense of hatred and fear. He admitted that he, too, had lived with a deep sense of hatred and resentment, until he moved in with an Israeli roommate during his college years. Suddenly, the Other had a name; he liked his coffee with milk but no sugar; and he shared similar dreams of one day settling down and starting a family of his own. This college roommate became his first Israeli friend and, more importantly, showed him that it was possible to transcend great divisions.

After he finished speaking, we sat together in a long, shared silence. Suddenly we were more than a group of newly acquainted young sustainability leaders. We had broken through, amidst all the sensory clatter of our first night in India, into something deeper.

This experience of "something deeper" moved us to reflect on the moments of connection that had influenced our own lives. We all had at least one key experience that had managed to break through the sediment of daily life and widen our circle of compassion while deepening our experience of the world. Indeed these were often the moments that had set a course in our lives that we were still trying to follow, and that had moved us to work for some purpose greater than ourselves. These were the moments that had opened up the possibility for transformative change to occur.

A week after our first meeting in Ahmedabad, we decided to launch a joint project—a global call for submissions celebrating moments of transformative connection. Since the launch of the call, we have received hundreds of submissions from countries around the world, from authors and photographers aged 11 to 82 years old. Although we can only share a small selection here, we remain deeply humbled and moved by the response.

What follows are stories and photos that speak to moments of interconnection and transformation. Some reflect global happenings or were gathered from prominent sustainability leaders, while others speak to small everyday moments, or were submitted by ordinary people with stories to share. While every moment is unique, all reflect on universal themes of human connection. We have organized the book around these universal themes: feeling a sense of place and belonging; encountering the wildness of nature; relating to the element of spirit in oneself or the world; experiencing an empathy that leaps across boundaries of difference; and, finally, being moved by shared joy or a simple celebration of renewed life.

Three years after the launch of this project, the vision of the Earth Charter that initially brought us together seems more relevant than ever. The principles of the Earth Charter sound our aspirations for our world and ourselves today, as well as a vision for what our future might be. At the heart of it all, is the vital recognition of our interconnectedness as part of one "earth community"; a call to return to our foundational connection to the world.

"Let ours be a time remembered for the awakening of a new reverence for life, the firm resolve to achieve sustainability, the quickening of the struggle for justice and peace, and the joyful celebration of life."—THE EARTH CHARTER

Two Pashtu elders share a laugh in the Paktia Province of Afghanistan.
photo by michal przedlacki

CHAPTER 1

At Home on Earth

Roots

When I was a child I loved listening to the birds around our homestead and learning their names. One particular bird sang at dusk and had a very special call that sounded like "ikia ngu, ikia ngu, ikia ngu," which translates as "toss the firewood." When I asked my mother what the bird was saying, she told me it was warning us: it is getting dark, so it's time to bring the firewood into the house. When I visit the countryside today, I still hear that bird, although not as often as I did when I was a child and there were more forests. However, when I do, I remember with delight what my mother told me. When children communicate with adults they learn a lot as they grow.

Collecting firewood for the household was a frequent activity and I would often help my mother do it. The country was dotted with hundreds of huge migumo, or wild fig trees, their bark the color of elephant skin and thick, gnarled branches with roots springing out and anchoring the tree to the ground. Fig trees had great green canopies beneath which grew dense undergrowth. This tree's canopy was probably sixty feet in diameter and it produced numerous fruits that birds loved. When the fruit was ready you would find hundreds of birds feeding on them. The undergrowth of the fig tree was also very fertile because people did not cut anything near those trees but allowed the undergrowth to flourish. All this added to the tree's mystery.

When my mother told me to go and fetch firewood, she would warn me, "Don't pick any dry wood out of the fig tree, or even around it." "Why?" I would ask. "Because that's a tree of God," she'd reply. "We don't use it. We don't cut it. We don't burn it." As a child, of course, I had no idea what my mother was talking about, but I obeyed her.

About two hundred yards from the fig tree there was a stream named Kanungu, with water so clean and fresh that we drank it straight from the stream. As a child, I used to visit the point where the water bubbled up from the belly of the earth to form a stream. I imagine

A group of children play on a fallen tree in the Toli-Toli region of Central Sulawesi, Indonesia. photo by thomas suryono

very few people have been lucky enough to see the source of a river. At the point where the stream came out of the ground, were planted arrowroots, and along the stream were banana plants, and sugarcane, which were typical food crops. Arrowroots, when cooked, provide a starchy tuber like potatoes, and grow only where there is a lot of water. At that time they were planted all along the banks of small, slow-flowing streams. Their large, deep green, arching leaves provided a hideaway big enough for a small child such as me to sit underneath. When it rained the silver drops of water would dance on the broad fronds above me and cascade to the ground. We also used these leaves to fetch water from the river and drink it. The water looked so clean and fresh against the sparkling green leaves.

Underneath the arrowroots, there would be thousands of frogs' eggs. They were black, brown, and white beads that I thought would make a beautiful necklace. I would spend hours trying to pick them up as gently as I could, hoping that I could put them around my neck. However, each time I placed my fingers below to lift them, the jelly that held them together would break and they would slip through my fingers back into the stream. I was so disappointed!

Time and time again I would return to that stream to play with the frogs' eggs. Suddenly

the eggs would disappear and subsequently I would see what seemed to be an army of black tadpoles wriggling in the water. I would try to catch them by their tails but they, too, were elusive. In time, these also would disappear and later on I would see many frogs hopping

The well-worn hands of a worker gather dates in the Taroudant Souk in southern Morocco.
photo by luca gargano

around the area near the stream. However, I never made the connection between the eggs, the tadpoles, and the frogs until I went to school and learned about the life cycle of amphibians. In my mind's eye I can envision that stream now: the crystal-clear water washing over the pebbles and grains of soil underneath, silky and slow moving. I can see the life in that water and the shrubs, reeds, and ferns along the banks, swaying as the current of the water sidles around them. When my mother would send me to fetch water, I would get lost in this fascinating world of nature until she would call out, "What are you doing under the arrowroots? Bring the water!"

I later learned that there was a connection between the fig tree's root system and the underground water reservoirs. The roots burrowed deep into the ground, breaking through the rocks beneath the surface soil and diving into the underground water table. The water traveled up along the roots until it hit a depression or weak place in the ground and gushed out as a spring. Indeed, wherever these trees stood, there were likely to be streams. The reverence the community had for the fig tree helped preserve the stream and the tadpoles that so captivated me. The trees also held the soil together, reducing erosion and landslides. In such ways, without conscious or deliberate effort, these cultural and spiritual practices contributed to the conservation of biodiversity...

Trees have been an essential part of my life and have provided me with many lessons. Trees are living symbols of peace and hope. A tree has roots in the soil yet reaches to the sky. It tells us that in order to aspire we need to be grounded, and that no matter how high we go it is from our roots that we draw sustenance. It is a reminder to all of us who have had success that we cannot forget where we came from. It signifies that no matter how powerful we become in government or how many awards we receive, our power and strength and our ability to reach our goals depend on the people, those whose work remains unseen, who are the soil out of which we grow, the shoulders on which we stand.

"Roots" comprises two excerpts by Wangari Maathai from her memoir, *Unbowed* (2006), published by Alfred A. Knopf, a division of Random House, Inc. New York. Reprinted with permission from the publishers. Pp. 44-46 and p. 293

Nature In and Around Me

I was raised in the midst of nature, 460 kilometers north of the Arctic Circle in the Northern Finnish village of Utsjoki. We Sami children were used to being outdoors. Our house was located near a big salmon-river, and nearby there were many good lands with lichen for reindeer. My parents owned reindeer, as well as sheep, and a horse for transport.

When I turned five, I knew something exciting was going to happen in my life. It was the first time that I would follow my parents and the rest of the family to a marsh area on a mountain plateau, at the distance of about 20 kilometers from our home. I knew from the stories of my parents that the lands we were soon to travel through were the lands of my ancestors. On our way to the marsh, we passed two sacred places. At the age of five, I was not yet familiar with sacred rocks, but I had heard that some Sami left antlers and coins there, and I understood that the ancestors manifest themselves somehow for people. We were quiet all the time during our trip: there were no loud voices, no wows. As I started writing this story, I asked my oldest sister how this journey was, according to her. She said that there was nothing special about these trips, and during that specific trip we mainly focused on the cloudberries. I told her that I remember the trip in a different way. It was a big event for me to come to the cloudberry lands and to stay there with my family. But it is true that we did not expect much to happen, and that we were used to receiving whatever came along.

During our trip, we made fire from dry juniper twigs and dwarf birch. There we sat in the midst of berries drinking coffee: we had fresh bread, salted salmon, dried reindeer meat, and homemade butter to eat. And, of course, we had cloudberries. There was a small lake where I fished trout while others picked berries. I did not catch any fish, but it was not important. To pass my time I also listened to frogs. We children were not allowed to play with them. Mother said that the Frog ancestor gets easily angry if frogs are disturbed. We slept in tents.

An Inuit girl enjoys a head massage from one of her new sled dog puppies in Kulusuk, Greenland. photo by ville miettinen

In the evenings, we could see stars between the clouds.

As a child, wolves visited me in my dreams, and I had frightening feelings about these early appearances. During my first night in the mountains, the wolves came back to my night visions, but not as before. In the dream, I came upon wolves near my parents' house, and as I passed them, I noticed that the pack was watching me. Some wolves were young, and they were playing with each other. I felt then that these animals were our longstanding family friends.

One evening, my mother talked about the reindeer and how she used to herd them as a young girl on these Kaldoaivi lands. My father joined in with other stories of the reindeer. As our journey continued, I kept on thinking of the wide reindeer eyes and the paths reindeer make. The next day, I felt a mysterious urge to take the role of a deer, and with a piece of antler in hand, to follow its path for a while.

As I grew older, I realized that these would be among the memories that I would carry with me into the future, and they would forever influence my thinking about the environment and my place in this world. To this day, the image of these vast lands has followed me, as nature in and around me.

A climber pauses to take in a vivid sunset while looking out over the mountain 'Presten' (The Priest) in the Lofoten Islands of Northern Norway.
photo by mina jokivirta

A group of women gather together to prepare a meal of potatoes and coleslaw in a Falukani community in the Altiplano region of Bolivia.
photo by david stephenson

ADITI RAO • INDIA

I Can Bear It

I spent the summer of 2007 as part of a volunteer group that was helping to build rainwater harvesting tanks, while supporting a local women's organization, and engaging in intense cultural exchanges in the Nahuatl indigenous village of Zoatecpan, Mexico. For seven weeks, I lived in a world where running water was non-existent, where I could knock on a stranger's door and be almost certain of a warm welcome and a delicious meal, where I never woke up to blaring traffic but often to the sound of dogs breaking into our room and eating our food. I learned to change my clothes inside a sleeping bag for want of any other private space, to hitchhike in open trucks on winding mountain roads without getting carsick, and to find absolute peace sitting on a rock and losing myself in the stars above and the clouds below.

Some weeks into the summer, though, I was struggling. I was part of, and had been asked to facilitate, a group of nine volunteers from four countries; we were living in the same room and sharing all our chores but were not yet able to resolve, or sometimes even recognize, the differences that arose between us. In my head, I was straddling four languages—English, Hindi, Spanish, and Nahuatl—and experiencing something of an identity crisis. I was also quite unwell and could not handle the manual work I had signed up for. Meanwhile, back home in India, on another planet, my grandfather was dying.

Slowly, the tiny threads that had bound my life together seemed to snap, and different pieces—my family in India, my illness, my college life in the USA, this adventure I had taken on in Mexico—weren't holding together anymore. I felt as if someone had ripped out the threads of a beautiful patchwork, revealing mere rags randomly placed together.

It was that same week that my team had decided to work harder on our relationship with the village community. Another team member and I had promised to go to a local family's house that night to learn how to make tortillas. Now, the last thing I wanted to be doing that particular night was make tortillas! But I had made a promise, so I went.

We walked into the small mud hut, and seated ourselves in the kitchen. A small light bulb hung in one corner, and our hostess showed us how to light the wood stove most efficiently. She handed out cups of steaming atolé, then pulled out the dough and began making tortillas. She was a traditional Nahuatl lady and wouldn't hear of letting her guests

work, even though that was why we had come there! So we sat on her floor and talked to the rhythmic beat of her hands as she slapped the dough into perfect circles.

Her 4 year-old grandson, who loved chattering endlessly in an adorable mix of Spanish and Nahuatl, heard our voices and came into the room: he too wanted tortillas and atolé. He snuggled up to me and sat there for a while, slurping the sweet milky drink and messily scooping up the sticky rice at the bottom of his mug. Then he rushed to the other room and brought in his older brother as well. His mother, with her one-year-old daughter, soon

After a long, hot December, this community on the outskirts of Lusaka, Zambia is waiting for the rainy season to start when rain suddenly bursts from the sky.
photo by shannon walsh

followed. Then the father came home from work, and we had a little party of eight, sitting around a simple wood stove in a mud thatched kitchen, and drinking hot atolé.

Dioselena, the baby girl, overcame her wariness of strangers and crawled up to me. Four-year-old Noah clung to me from one side, and his older brother Israel, determined not to be left out, pulled my hair from the other. I bounced all three children around, laughing, as their parents and grandmother looked on. I threw the little girl into the air and caught her, over and over, until she couldn't stop giggling. The two little boys fought over more atolé and offered me fresh, hot tortillas from the stove. Their parents chatted about life in the village, the beauty of the corn crop, and the fights that their sons got into. By now, the room was too warm and filled with smoke from the open stove, but the soft light and the genuine enjoyment of one another's company kept us from being uncomfortable. What was intended as a 30-minute tortilla-making lesson turned into three hours of laughter over a simple meal.

Later, as Noah and I were resting on our way to the schoolhouse where my team and I were living, the little boy confided that he planned to go back to my country with me. When I asked him if he wouldn't miss home and his family, he was silent for a long moment. Then he replied bravely, "Sí, pero aguanto" ("Yes, but I'll bear it").

With that child's declaration, all differences of culture, economic class, nationality, gender, and age faded away. Suddenly, we were just two human beings, enjoying each other's company, bound together by the simple joy of play. My own identity crisis as I struggled between languages and cultures, all the conflicts within my team, and even my need to be with my family in a hard moment, faded into the gentle knowledge that it was all okay because, at the end of the day, we are all in this together.

In the seven weeks I spent in Zoatecpan, I learned more about life and love and myself than I had imagined possible in one summer. And the defining moment of my stay there is simply the memory of a four-year-old boy sitting with me on a rock, with miles and miles of cornfields around us, telling me that he can bear leaving behind everything he knows in order to be with me. That boy and that moment will forever bind me to Zoatecpan, to the Mexican countryside, and to every child and every adult in every part of the world who knows the joy of play.

24

The eye of a young plains zebra, photographed during the rainy season in South Africa's Kruger National Park.
photo by pim stouten

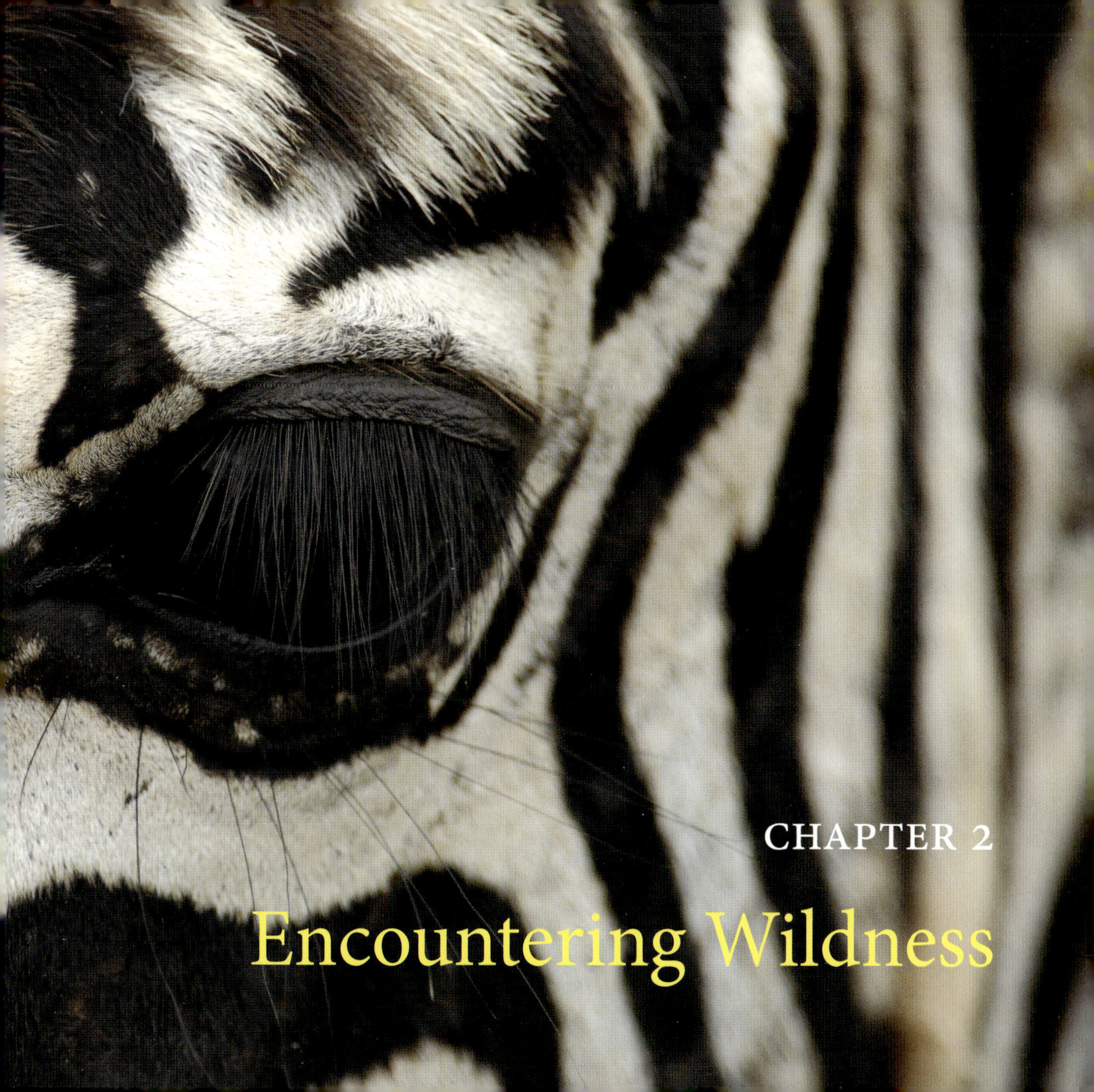

CHAPTER 2

Encountering Wildness

A. JAMES WOHLPART • USA

Encountering Wildness

Many years ago, during a difficult time in my life, I would tell a story of an encounter with a rattlesnake. At that time, the story revealed to me the many disjunctions and disharmonies that existed in my life. It offered evidence that a life that had gone awry could return to its source, a place of relation and perhaps humility.

In the telling of the story, I explained how I had taken a day for myself, away from the commitments and obligations of family and work and the all-consuming materialism of our culture. I drove to Myakka River State Park with my trail bike and daypack in tow. I arrived shortly after the park opened, studied the bike trail map, and found a place where I thought I could spend some time in wildness, alone.

I rode for about three hours on sandy roads that meandered through pine uplands. The immense sky caused me to ache as I reflected on the many hours spent locked in my office or keeping up a house twice the size of my grandparents' home. The sun rose and the day warmed. I ran out of water and so I headed back to the car, thinking that I would get my lunch and my daypack and retreat back into wildness to eat and nap.

As I put my bike into the car and prepared my lunch, a pair of red-shouldered hawks screamed at me from the top of nearby pine trees.

I was at a point in my life when I thought that I had awakened and, interestingly, hawks had been an integral part of this awakening experience. I felt that I had become aware of the way in which life's meaninglessness, its routines, its habits, the shallowness of work and a consumer culture, can overwhelm and take you under to the point where all you know is this meaningless state. To the point where the routines, the work, and the consumption become a never ending cycle of feeling the void, then filling the void with things, only to feel empty again. We have come to mistake this cycle for a meaningful journey, a rite-of-passage. It has become our vision quest in Western culture, where young adults roam mega-malls in the desire to become.

A hunter and his eagle companion in the capital of Ulaanbaatar during the 800th anniversary of the Mongolian nation. photo by hans hendriksen

A spider slowly weaves its web on an early autumn day in the countryside of Sipoo, southern Finland.
photo by tomi nytorp

In this dire state, red-shouldered hawks spoke to me, reminding me of a time in my life when I had a direct connection to wildness, a strong sense of humility, an awareness of solitude. They had provided a foundation for a sense of interrelatedness with all things. Not just other humans, but rocks and trees and birds and animals, the clouds, the sky, the sun, the moon, the stars.

So I knew what they were saying, these hawks that were screaming at me from the tops of the slash pines above my car. "Don't go! Danger! Don't go!" But I was new to this listening and didn't believe what I heard, didn't believe that the hawks had a message for me. I packed my lunch and headed down the wilderness trail.

I walked for about an hour in a hushed forest of slash pine. The trail meandered through an understory of saw palmetto, wax myrtle and ferns. I came to a camping area and went to the most isolated spot furthest from the trail. No one was there. I opened my lunch and ate, then lay down for a nap.

I was in the shade of an ancient live oak, one hundred feet tall with broad limbs. Some of the limbs bowed down to the ground in an elegant semblance of thanksgiving, some of them rose up like arms honoring the heavens. The wind blew through the oak, the leaves dancing in the breeze.

As I lay on the ground, I slowly drifted into a deep and comfortable sleep. I was more relaxed than I had been in years; the cares of life had fallen away and left me raw, exposed, unhurried. As I fell into this peaceful state, I was absorbed into Earth, a giant soft hand lowering me into a new realm away from the cares and worries of this life: a sacred place of stillness and peace.

I don't know how long I slept, perhaps thirty minutes, but I awoke very suddenly, coming fully out of my sleep to a state of heightened alertness. I turned my head to the left. A fully-grown, thick-bodied diamond-backed rattlesnake stared at me, some twelve inches from my nose.

Interestingly, I did not panic. A shaft of light streamed through the live oak, warming my stomach. In the time that I lay there face to face with the snake, I had a strong sense that the snake wanted to climb on my belly, curl up, and take a nap.

After a time—I don't know how long, for time had seemed to stop—I was overwhelmed with a sense of the danger confronting me. I rolled away from the snake, and stood up.

From my new vantage point, I got a better look at the snake, which was over four feet long with beautiful diamonds spaced down its back. It watched me for a moment and then slowly made its way into the saw palmettos.

The story as I told it for years was one of triumph, of a life that had gone awry because of a dulling of the senses, from work and obligations and hyper-consumption, but that was now back on track. After all, the hawks had warned me of this dangerous encounter that I was about to have.

But many years have passed since those tellings. In that time, I have read and learned much, and this has helped me realize how much more I have yet to learn. In my reading, I encountered an essay called *The Snake People* by Chickasaw writer Linda Hogan. In the essay she explains that our Western view of snakes as a representation of darkness and evil does not fit with the view of native peoples. She notes, "Before Snake became the dark god of our underworld, burdened with human sin, it carried a different weight in our human bones; it was a being of holy inner earth… In nearly all ancient cultures the snake was a symbol of healing and wholeness."

Now, when I tell the story of my encounter with the rattlesnake, I am less sure of its significance, just as I am less certain of the hawks' message. Perhaps they were not warning me of any danger. Perhaps they were letting me know that I was not yet ready to understand this encounter with wildness, that I was still in need of healing and wholeness.

Perhaps if I had been able to lay still long enough to let the snake climb on my belly in the warming sun, perhaps for a short time, I might have been cradled by this holy Earth.

The quotation is drawn from: Linda Hogan (1995), *Dwellings: A Spiritual History of the Living World*, published by Touchstone, New York. P. 140.

This tree stands strong as the remaining one on a hill overlooking the Ibitipoca State Park in the municipality of Lima Duarte, Brazil. photo by marcelo eduardo salgado

Help

Back in the nineties, I found myself going through the routine that many twenty–some-things in North America often do, that rite of passage of working two jobs to barely cover rent and food, living pay check to pay check, and often relying on the kindness of others to get by. My rent money was paid to my saint of a best friend and her brother and sister who shared a house in London, Ontario, and this bought me a cubby space at the foot of the basement stairs into which I squeezed my futon and a dresser. Despite my tight quarters, I was extremely grateful for my little mouse hole, because it housed me and my beloved dog, and because my housemates were people who loved me. And of course, it's always love that makes life bearable.

Unfortunately, it didn't always feel bearable. I got up at 6:00 a.m. so that my highly energetic dog could pull me around the neighborhood for half an hour, and then I got ready and rushed downtown to begin my first job at 8:00 a.m. I worked until noon, when I would catch a bus home, wolf down a lunch, pack a dinner, run out the door with my dog for another 20 minutes, and then race back out to catch yet another bus across town to job number two. This job ended at 11:00 p.m. I would then catch a final bus back home, crash into sleep on my futon in my mouse hole by 12:30 a.m., and start all over the next day.

Now, I want to be very clear here   I know that compared to countless people in many countries around the world, I was living a good life. I wasn't starving on the streets. I was safe at night. I had two jobs. But after a few months of non-stop running, you start to get a little tired. Even in your twenties.

Inevitably then, there came a day. Actually, there came a moment, in the middle of the second dog walk, in the glow of a beautiful sunny day along the banks of London's Thames River, when I suddenly felt tired. And of course, it wasn't just "tired". It was like when you're swimming in the ocean and you're so busy jumping and laughing in the waves that you forget to watch out, and then just as

A boy from the Pataxós tribe holds his pet, a three-toed sloth, in the state of Bahia, Brazil. photo by marcelo eduardo salgado

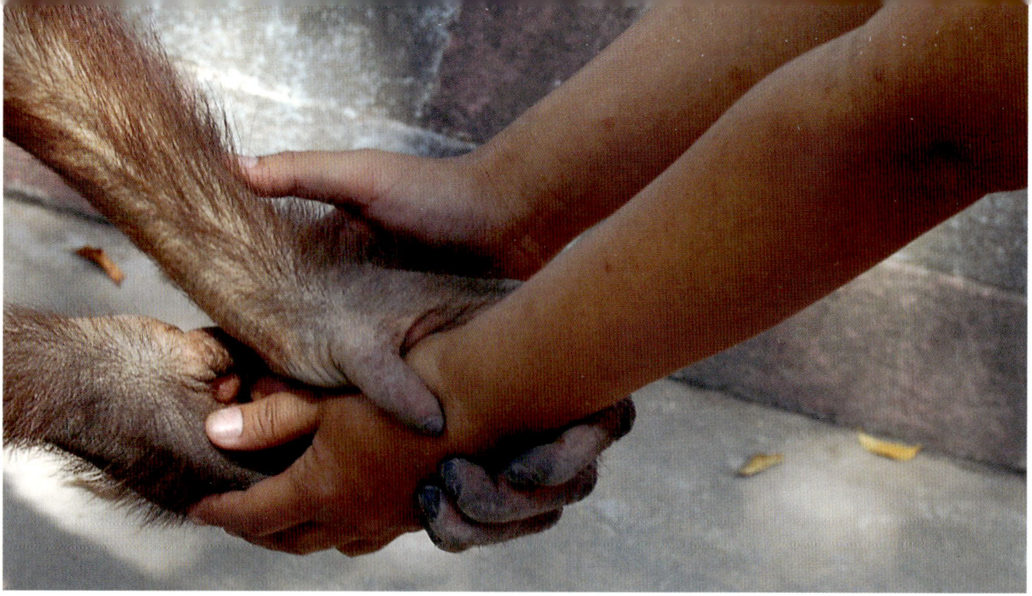

you're waving at your friends—WHAMMO!—a big old wave hits you right in the back of the head and slams you under the water. It rolls you around, and in your surprise you think for a moment, "Oh my God, I might actually drown here!" That is what it was like. There I was, speed walking my dog along the river trail, and WHAMMO! A giant wave of absolute exhaustion hit me from behind and almost rolled me over. My limbs felt weak, I couldn't catch my breath, and it felt too hard to take one more step. I felt like I was drowning.

I actually had to stop walking. I just stood there in the middle of the trail, with my dog looking at me with that, "What's up?" expression on her face, and I couldn't go one more step. I took a deep breath, the kind I had learned in yoga class to center myself and gain control. And that's when the tears came. I fought them off valiantly, but they welled up anyway, and I stood there feeling weak and sad and unsure of what to do next. So, I did what most people probably do when they're drowning—I asked for help.

"Help," I said in my head. It wasn't a yell; I was too tired even for that. It was simply a pure, direct request of the universe at large. And it wasn't just a word, though the word did form in my head. It was also a feeling, an ache; a need that I felt in every cell of my body. I had no idea what kind of help I was asking for. Maybe a kind, professional dog walker who

An orangutan and a visitor share a moment of connection at the Gembiraloka Zoo in the city of Yogyakarta, Indonesia. photo by tri silvanto

would see me standing there in tears and offer to walk my dog twice a day for free? That could help. Or maybe a stellar job offer that would come my way – perhaps the CBC needed a First Nations writer to join a team that was writing and producing plays and my material was just what they were looking for, big pay checks included? That could definitely help. I didn't know what I meant exactly, just that I couldn't go on as I was. Despite having been hit by a wave, my well was dry.

It was then, hearing a noise, that I looked up into just the help I needed. Bright and massive, its red-tufted head diligently drilling into the rough bark of a giant oak tree, a pileated woodpecker caught my eye and in that same instant, my heart. Beautiful and unexpected, the sight of this woodpecker washed away fatigue and helplessness like a rain shower. I was firmly caught. Transfixed in its strength and vibrancy. And, though it may sound odd, I felt a connection to this bird that was as strong as the love I feel for my own family. I have since realized that this was because this bird was part of my family, a connection to everything I know about my world and all of the mysteries that I do not know. Through this bird, for the briefest of moments, I was given the gift of a strong message that I felt rather than heard—that I was not alone, and someone was listening.

My response was profound. "Oh!" I said. What else can you say when you feel like something from the beyond has just reached out and tapped you on the shoulder? I stood, rooted like the oak tree, admiring the bird's strong beak and feet, drinking in the sheen of the ebony feathers, savoring the tingle I felt in every nerve. I was not alone, and someone was listening.

My dog grew restless at the end of her leash. I didn't want to leave my woodpecker and this moment in my life, but the seconds on my watch were ticking by, and my dog would not wait. Life would not wait. So I stayed as long as I could, and then I walked on. Knowing I was being listened to was enough; I found the energy to take the next step and keep going.

The woodpecker has since become one of my animal helpers in life; I never fail to see one when I am at a crossroads or asking again for help. As an Anishnaabe woman living in this modern, technology-filled world, they are a comforting reminder to me that we are all related—people, dogs, trees, rivers, woodpeckers. And even now when I am fortunate enough to live in a house with multiple rooms, and have one job that pays the bills, I am grateful every day for the challenges of that time in my life, and for the help that came as a result.

The mountain seems to take a breath during the photographer's alpine ascent to Chopicalqui, in the Peruvian Andes. photo by juan carlos pina

MICHAEL J. COHEN • USA

Earth Alive

A spectacle of cliffs and color mark the place where Bright Angel Creek joins the Colorado River deep in the bowels of Grand Canyon National Park, five thousand feet below the rim. The canyon's multi-billion year old granite-veined schists portray the birth and changes of ancient landscapes and life. Here, on a scorching day in 1967, a group of kids, some critical thinking, a thunderstorm and a bag of potato chips cracked my thick walls of consciousness about life and the land.

The summer expedition group that I was leading was on a three-day backpacking trip into Grand Canyon's inner gorge. Early that morning the red star, Antares, had brightly shone on our frost-covered sleeping bags at the canyon's nine thousand foot rim, but by mid-afternoon the inner canyon temperature, a mile below, simmered at nearly 120 degrees Fahrenheit or 48 degrees Celsius. To keep cool I hiked without a shirt on. Occasionally, I munched a potato chip to maintain my body's salt level in the broiling desert. Touching my bare stomach as I walked the suspension bridge that crosses the muddy Colorado River, I was surprised to find that though I was hot, my stomach felt extremely cold. I touched my arm and it, too, felt memorably icy.

Now a scientific person like myself has learned to explain the coolness generated by sweating through molecular theory: Due to the sun's intensity, both the desert and my body heat up. However, in order to maintain its life-sustaining temperature, my body sweats, transferring its heat to sweat molecules, making them more active. They become vibrant enough to evaporate and jump off my body into the air, carrying away with them excess body heat while leaving a residue of salt on my skin.

With the molecular theory's explanation firmly in mind, I continued my journey through the canyon, giving the matter no second thought. It was a "small" matter in the infinite scheme of things. It had never occurred to me that I was engaged in a miraculous event that kept me temperate while the rocks burned. I never wondered how my body knew when to sweat, when to stop sweating or how this information grew, was communicated or enacted.

While we rested at Bright Angel Creek's junction with the Colorado River, I noticed storm clouds moving in from the southwest. "Now you're going to see something amazing," I told the expedition members. "As that thunderstorm pours, the raindrops will evaporate in the atmosphere's heat before they reach us here on the canyon floor. We'll watch the rain fall upon us, but we won't get wet."

I knew that this fun thing was going to happen. It had happened many times before when I camped in the Grand Canyon. A few expedition folks were skeptical, but all were excited by the prospect of the upcoming "dry storm."

The dark clouds came, and sure enough, they began to pour down torrents that drenched us to the bone while we stood there agape! "Hey, look everybody, I'm really dry,." taunted one very wet young girl as she and the rest of the smirking group members scurried for raincoats and cover.

"Oh sure, Mike, it never rains in the Grand Canyon." How often those words would assail me that summer and in the years to come. Somehow, every student I worked with heard about the incident, and each felt moved to remind me of the event whenever I came close to suggesting what might soon take place. If I announced that we would have eggs for breakfast, the first response was, "Sure and it never rains in the Grand Canyon." I couldn't even read tomorrow's tide or sunrise table without hearing not one, but a chorus of voices, blurt, "Sure, Mike, and it never rains in the Grand Canyon." Even today when I hear politicians and industrialists state how more nukes will produce peace, or how new toxins won't get into my water or food, I say, "Right! And it never rains in the Grand Canyon."

But the sky had opened up and rain it did. Quickly, the canyon had cooled. And, like soap rinsed out of your hair, the red sands and clays of the Grand Canyon sloshed over the steep, thousand-foot black cliffs. All these sediments and salts run down into the sea. Why doesn't the sea become increasingly salty? From natural erosion the ocean doubles its salt content every ninety million years. Why, after its many billion years' existence, isn't the ocean saltier than the lifeless Great Salt Lake in Utah? Does the ocean have some kind of kidney? Does the Earth sweat away salt like my body? Were these foolish questions? Were they just small things? They didn't seem to be.

The canyon's radical temperature change also brought to mind my cold, perspiring skin during the hike, just moments before I had wondered: Can the Planet become too hot or too cold for life to exist? Wasn't the Earth cooling itself by evaporating moisture the same way my body had cooled itself? If the Planet reacts like a living organism, does it also regulate its

Fishing in a rice paddy in Vang Vieng, Laos. photo by ben visbeek

oxygen and carbon dioxide content, as would another life form? If the Planet practices homeostasis and reacts like a living organism, does that mean that it is a living organism?

Earth as a living organism? Although I had enjoyed this daydream, I felt concerned about where my mind was going. Maybe the heat was getting to me and a salt pill was in order. An occasional, "Hey, Mike, it never rains in the Grand Canyon," did nothing to help my self-credibility. To mention my Living Earth thoughts to others was the last thing on my mind. After all, it did rain in the Grand Canyon!

Had I been living in some human-created environment, the matter would probably have ended, relegated to the definition of daydream. But I was in the wilderness where Mother Nature continued to smile at me, and over the years she blew life into that spark of storm-ignited Living Earth consciousness. The laughing wind fanned the spark. An ember formed whose flame cooked up still more heated questions and inner conflict. "Was the Earth actually self-regulating and alive?" became a burning issue. The fire grew, as fuel for thought was added by both old memories and new experiences. What began as an academic conflict, grew in scope and importance, and has led me to found schools, degree programs and symposiums around this question. It became for me a key to rectifying our posture toward the natural world, each other and ourselves.

Children in Bangladesh participate in the Thousand Lantern Lighting, a ritual whereby every full moon month Buddhists light 1,000 lanterns for the welfare of humanity.
photo by mohammad rakibul hasan

CHAPTER 3

Honoring the Spirit

Forest Temple

After an especially cold winter in Edmonton, I accepted a position at the University of British Columbia, in Vancouver, in 1963, returning at last to the city of my birth. With a young family, I repeated the example of my parents, planning camping and fishing trips for my children so that they could experience nature. Every weekend, we would try to get out into a new area, following leads provided by others, driving along country and logging roads around Vancouver to reach isolated rivers and lakes.

I had been at UBC for about a year when I heard about a logging road near Squamish that would take us to a river that was supposed to contain good-sized rainbow trout. So one Sunday, I loaded my children, Tamiko and Troy, into the car and took off for a day trip. Passing Squamish, we left the pavement for a dirt road and soon encountered a sign announcing that we were entering forest company land, where logging trucks had the right of way. The road was in excellent condition and wound through the hills for kilometers. In the area being actively logged, the forest had been cleared and the debris that was left gathered up into great piles to be burned. Having spent most of my life in the east, I wasn't especially disturbed by the logging; after all, I loved working with wood in carpentry and used a lot of paper at work, and I knew that forestry was the engine of the B.C. economy. Besides, the logging roads enabled me to get into remote parts of the province.

When the road finally neared the river, I drove up a hill and found a level spot on the shoulder. We put on our daypacks, picked up our fishing gear, and set off. All around us was a combat zone where the soil had been churned up by the tracks of heavy machines, and all that remained of the immense trees were huge stumps and roots that projected at garish angles among the slash. From the top of the hill, the logged-out clearing had looked deceptively smooth and easy to traverse, but once we had left the roadside and started to descend the hill, it became tough slogging to get by the debris. Time after time, I was forced to

The beauty and remoteness of Hornby Island, off the West Coast of Canada, invite contemplation. photo by edward butterworth

hoist the children up over obstructions. What I had thought would be an easy ten-minute hike turned into an hour, but once committed, I wasn't about to give up. I kept bantering with the children and playing games with them as we worked our way across the clearing. I was far too focused on the challenge of traversing the clearing to reflect on the fact that this was a war zone where human economic demands were conflicting with the continuation of the community of life making up the ecosystem.

It was a sunny day and I soon found myself sweating profusely, kicking myself for not bringing any water and worrying about the children. After much puffing and unjamming of the rods I was carrying from branches and debris, we finally reached the trees at the edge of the logged area. Stepping out of the glare and heat of the clearing and into the dark, cool cathedral of trees was an absolute shock, like stepping from a hot city street into an air-conditioned building. Embraced by the cool shade of the trees, we inhaled the damp, musky odour of vegetation and decaying tree carcasses.

We were enfolded in silence. The children immediately stopped bickering and complaining and began to whisper just as if they were in a church. As our eyes adjusted to the shade, we saw that the forest floor was cloaked with moss that smoothed everything into an undulating carpet. The bodies of great leviathans of fallen trees could be seen in outline under the moss, in death nurturing a community of huckleberry, sword ferns, and small trees. As we searched for a trickle of water to drink, the cracking of branches under our feet was muffled by the vegetation. High above us, the canopy stretched to the sky with green branches and needles jockeying for a place in the sun and allowing an ever-shifting filigree of speckled light onto the forest floor. As terrestrial creatures, we could only wonder at the drama of life cycles and predation taking place in the nooks and crannies of the branch tips, needles, and leaves of the canopy and in the soil community hidden beneath our feet. Tamiko, Troy, and I joined hands and reached around the circumference of one of the trees, not even reaching halfway around. Those giants must have been hundreds of years old.

I was dumbstruck. Nature had always been my touchstone, but I had spent much of my life in Ontario, where forests had been heavily impacted and altered by people. There trees had been extracted, creeks rerouted, and the soil cultivated or developed. This was a forest shaped by the forces of nature for ten thousand years, a community of life where death gave birth to new life in an endless recycling of nutrients through the countless species that make up a forest. We had stepped into it from the edge of industrial logging, which would soon

A Maori warrior embraces his son after participating in a cultural celebration carrying forth the ancestral tradition of the haka. photo by clayton jay scott

transform it into something infinitely simplified and unrecognizable.

In those few minutes that my children and I had entered into the forest temple, I had recognized the terrible hubris of the human economy. To transform this matrix of life forms, soil, water and air into a war zone where soil, air, water and life were so degraded was a travesty of stewardship and responsibility to future generations. I didn't articulate it in that way at the time. I only knew in a profoundly visceral way that industrial logging was not right, that the magnificent forest we had entered was an entity far beyond our comprehension and was worthy of respect and veneration.

I had been set up to have that inspirational encounter with an old-growth forest after reading Rachel Carson's seminal book, Silent Spring, in 1962. Years later, I would encounter First Nations people who would educate me about our kinship with other species and the way in which we are all interconnected and interdependent. But that encounter with an ancient forest on the edge of a clear-cut was my moment of enlightenment.

Today, when my grandchildren beg me to go fishing with them, I can't take them to Spanish Banks or the mouths of the Fraser or the Vedder River or other places where my father took me. I can't go back to fish in the Thames River, which is so polluted that people recoil at the thought of eating anything caught there. I can't return to the swamp that soothed me during my adolescence, for it is now covered with an immense shopping mall and parking lot. And the forest that was my epiphany was felled within weeks of my visit there. What remains is my conviction that we must discover our biological place and learn to live in balance with the natural world that sustains us.

"Forest Temple" comprises an excerpt from "Catching an Epiphany," by David Suzuki, found in the book *When the Wild Comes Leaping Up*, (2002) by David Suzuki, published by Greystone Books & the David Suzuki Foundation. Reprinted with permission from the publishers.

BLAIR BRAVERMAN • USA

Ice and Ashes

The summer I turned eighteen, I lived on a glacier. It was a broad, slanted finger of snow, a home I shared with two hundred huskies and a dozen people. From above, the camp was smudges on white, pressed against the base of a black mountain: canvas tents, ordered doghouses, trails that stretched into the fields beyond. I was working as a dogsled guide in Alaska, near Juneau. Each morning I would pull myself from my sleeping bag, slip on my raincoat and boots, and step from my tent into the pale light of the northern summer, the glacier luminous beneath me in the rising sun.

After chores—feeding the dogs, cleaning trails—a distant purr would echo over the mountains, and a line of helicopters grew in the sky until they were right above us, the air throbbing with the beat of their rotors. I waited by the sled while the birds landed, the handlebar jerking under my hand as the dogs jumped in excitement, and for one hour I would escort passengers on a tour, skimming across the ice field in gentle silence. Over the course of the summer I gave close to 700 tours; of these, one alone stands out.

On that tour I had a single passenger, an older woman with a southern accent and a creased face. As we left the kennel she told me her story: how she and her husband had always longed to visit Alaska's glaciers; how they had finally made it up, last year, only to be forced down in a sudden storm; how he had fallen ill—cancer—and passed away that winter. I listened, kicking snow with one foot as we slid along the trail.

"I'm sorry to hear that," I said.

She smiled. "Don't be. I'm glad to be here today."

Two miles in I paused to give my dogs a rest, a chance to bite snow and cool down. When the sled stopped, the woman pulled something from the folds of her coat: a sandwich bag filled with earthy powder. She pressed it to her heart for a moment, then leaned over the side of the sled basket, scooping at the snow with her free hand. Hurriedly, she

A majestic iceberg gazes from the shores of Griffith Island in the northernmost territory of Nunavut, Canada. photo by dave brosha

emptied the ashes into the hole, patted a handful of snow on top, and returned both hands to her lap like an attentive child. Her papery skin stretched tight across the knuckles of her clasped hands.

"Are the dogs ready yet?" she asked. "Let's keep going."

For the rest of the run, neither of us spoke. I doubt I could have. When the tour ended, I touched the woman's hand, then watched as she climbed into a helicopter and lifted into the sky. I wondered if I wasn't the only one watching her go.

Throughout the evening I was troubled. I realized that the next morning, when we cleaned the trails, the ashes would be collected with the other dirt, then packed into a barrel and flown to a Juneau sewage treatment center. This, after the woman had come such a long way. I went to my boss and told him of a plan I was forming, but he only shook his head. "This isn't your responsibility," he said. "It would be too dangerous. One dead body is enough for today—we don't want you hurt, too."

That night I couldn't sleep. He's right, I told myself. It's not my responsibility. But the longer I lay awake, the more I was certain of what had to be done. And so in the young hours of the morning, deeply uneasy, I stepped from my tent. It was overcast, and the mountains were contours, dark and still. In the kennel, a few dogs paced in the faint moonlight, collar tags jingling softly.

We kept three snowmobiles in camp and I started the smallest, wincing as its engine cut the night's silence. After a few minutes' driving I found the ashes, a gray-brown patch that seemed to pulse against the white trail. What had seemed so simple in the tent—to dig up the ashes and move them—seemed, suddenly, very difficult. And no one was allowed beyond the outermost path, which was where I planned to go; it was the only place where the ashes wouldn't be disturbed.

I closed my eyes and took a slow breath, feeling my lungs expand and cool with the night air, and as I exhaled, I reached down and dug my naked hands into the snow. The ashes were buried more deeply than I had expected, and I pulled them up in handfuls, gathering a dirty mound. My fingers stiffened with the cold and I breathed on them, trying to ignore the dark crescents jammed under the nails, trying to forget that they were part of a human body.

When I could move my hands again I began packing the pile together, carefully pressing the growing snowball into a perfect sphere, stained gray like frozen smoke. Then, lifting the ball to my chest, I stepped off the trail. Out here, crevasses waited blue and veiled under the surface, plunging like cracks to the center of the earth, and I walked cautiously, expecting to fall through with every step. When the burn of the snow in my palms forced me to stop, I looked back. I could no longer see the trail or the snowmobile; only my footprints broke the billowing expanse, a dotted line shrinking into the horizon.

I crouched down and placed the ball on the snow, wondering, reflecting. A man lives his life, falls in love and marries and dies, only to be carried by a stranger across a barren glacier in the Alaskan wilderness. His ashes would melt into the ice with the next rainfall, then creep downhill for a decade or more before calving into the sea in great white boulders. It struck me that I had never before felt this alone, here on an empty ice field under dark mountains, with the burden of leaving a man behind. It was as if I were packing part of myself into the snowball, as if I would emerge less than whole.

It seemed disrespectful not to provide some sort of ceremony, and I felt a sudden anger at the man's wife, his nameless loved ones, for leaving me—a stranger!—with the tremendous responsibility of the final goodbye. What could I possibly say that could do justice to an entire life lived, that could show compassion, kindness, understanding? I knew nothing, nothing at all about the man in my hands. I bit my lip until it stung, trying to think clearly. And then, cautiously, I began to speak.

"I never met you," I said, and my voice sounded thin in the sweeping silence, "but I think you were probably a good man. You were probably just like any of us, good sometimes but not always, just trying to be a better person. I bet you did things you were proud of and things you regretted, and you learned from your mistakes. There are people today whose lives are better because you were part of them. If you have kids, I'm sure they love you very much. I know your wife does." I swallowed. "She's probably in Juneau right now, thinking you're where she left you, and maybe that brings her peace."

I stood long in the clouded moonlight, thinking. I thought about what makes us human, our shared truths, our deepest hopes, the peace that comes from understanding that we are not alone. In the distance a soft howl rose and fell, trailing off so gradually that I couldn't tell when it ended, and after a moment I turned. As I walked towards the trail I felt the weight of tears on my cheeks, but when I reached up to brush them away, it was only snowflakes.

A shortened version of "Ice and Ashes" has previously been published in *Appalachia*, Summer/ Fall 2011 issue, p. 100.

A clown leads a group of children across a stretch of desert in the state of Rajasthan, India, near the border of Pakistan. photo by azli jamil

CHAPTER 4
Crossing Borders, Sharing Responsibility

Chanakuh—a Rabbi lights the menorah in Union Square, San Francisco, USA. photo by thomas hawk

In a Wink

It was in the squalor and beauty of the never-ending outskirts of New Delhi that I walked
  hand in hand with my dearest friend the Imam
  towards the assembled students of the madrasha
I was the first Jew they had ever encountered
Their eyes were narrowed, a gaze of apprehension, even fear,
  veiled in hatred
It tore my heart and the baby in me cried

When I was three months old I must have opened my eyes
When the Gestapo leader looked at me and said
What a pity that this is a Jewish child
My gaze had reached his heart and made him turn away and spare us
And so I know that as long as the eyes of a baby can still reach the heart
Though it might be overtaken by indoctrination
Nothing is lost

The stereotypes about the Jews hung in the air
A dark curtain of incomprehension
I groped for words to bridge the gap, my body and soul trembling
How my father had insisted on giving me the name shalom
In the midst of war-torn Amsterdam
Telling the reluctant registry officer
Shalom he will be called because shalom there will be

4B
ANAS

Then suddenly I thought to teach them the simple song of peace
We have brought you peace with the Hebrew words Shalom Aleechem
And the Arabic rendering Salaam Aleikum
And slowly they started to sing with me
And I saw the miracle happening, eyes opening fully
Every trace of anger, even hatred, disappeared
And it all happened in a whisper of time
When the heart opens everything is possible

A few years later in a gathering of spiritual leaders near the Lake of Galilee
The Imam told the tale of the eyes that had opened
I was sitting next to him deeply moved
We had never discussed this miraculous incident of hope
He had seen what I had seen
We truly shared the same language of revelation
When you hear the light and see the whisper
And it was this inner connectedness of brothers, Jewish and Muslim
That had helped the children to cross the border of enmity into love
In a wink

Two young students listen in on a lesson by Oluyemisi Joel-Osebor, a teacher and youth worker in Kano State, Nigeria.
photo by oluyemisi joel-osebor

HUSNUR ESTHIWAHYU • INDONESIA

Drawn Together by Disaster

"Are you a Javanese? Go back to your place! We hate you. We don't need help from you."

That was the greeting I received from a group of men when I arrived at one of the camps for internally displaced peoples in Banda Aceh, the capital city of Aceh Province. It was not exactly what I had expected when I decided to fly all the way to the westernmost part of Indonesia to help with earthquake and tsunami relief efforts.

I had been asked to come work at the camp two weeks after a 9.0 Richter scale earthquake followed by a tsunami hit the Indian Ocean on December 26th, 2004. The camp, which was erected inside a soccer stadium, was intended for outpatients and the families of those patients admitted to the nearby field hospital. These people were there so that they could easily commute back and forth to the field hospital. But most importantly, they were there because their houses had been destroyed by the tidal waves that had killed more than 160,000 people. Their hometowns were either under water, or full of mud and debris. All of the roads and bridges leading to those areas were wiped out. They had nowhere else to go.

The camp was not ready when I arrived. The men who had so unpleasantly greeted me turned out to be the workers in charge of putting up around 40 family tents, 4 even larger tents, a medical facility center, showers, toilets, and kitchens. As if I had said a wrong prayer, I found myself assigned to work with the 15 men who had seemingly hated me since the first time they had seen me there.

I do not know how I managed to mingle with them but day after day, slowly, these men started to share their stories with me. How the tsunami had taken their wives, children, parents, relatives, and all of the tools and materials they had for working in the forest or fishing in the sea. How they had suffered from the armed conflict between the Indonesian military and the Free Aceh Movement that had gone on

Community members help rebuild the home of Hazera Khatun after it was destroyed by a cyclone that inundated the low-lying area of Bangladesh.
photo by mohammad rakibul hasan

for more than 30 years; how the military had beaten them or brutally burned down their villages, and how people that they had known were among the 10,000 people who had died from the armed conflict. I learned that their hatred towards the Javanese stemmed from the fact that the Acehnese felt that they were occupied by the Javanese, the majority ethnic group in Indonesia, and that most of the Indonesian army personnel based in Aceh happened to be Javanese. Nevertheless, they also learned that the Javanese girl working side-by-side with them in the disaster relief efforts had a name and a smiling face. She was harmless, and wanting to be friends with them.

As a team, we tried to serve the displaced persons living in the camp. We shared the duties of distributing food items, blankets, lanterns, buckets and other basic necessities to those staying in the camp. We made a small swimming pool, seesaw, swing, and library to keep the children entertained. And we managed to find a way to call doctors and nurses on the radio in case of medical emergencies, even though many of us had very limited knowledge of English. "From camp…from camp…baby born…baby born…" was the most common emergency call. We gave welcoming celebrations every time newborns became our new camp members. In turn, they brought us all new energy and joy.

We also, however, came together around our fears. The armed conflict continued in some places beyond the camp. In the night, from our tents, we could hear the exchange of gunfire. Sometimes one or two military personnel intruded into the camp, causing everyone to go pale. Even the security guards, who were supposed to protect the camp from all intruders, could not hide the fear of another dreadful scene. What if the military personnel felt offended when they asked them to leave the camp? What if they took revenge later?

Yet they could not be left to roam the tents, looking for someone they suspected to be their foe. Someone had to talk to them. I had no war trauma, having grown up far from the brutal armed conflict. I also had a badge from the organization, which is supposed to provide protection in conflict areas. So I went to talk to the military personnel and explained that they were not supposed to be in the camp. The fact that the personnel and I were both Javanese did not help me feel safe; I did not think that they valued my being the same ethnic group as them. Nor did I have full confidence in the protection that the emblem and the international law could give to a humanitarian worker in this battleground. I, the tenants, and all camp workers, including the security guards, shared the same fear of what violence might still lie ahead.

We also shared the fear of another earthquake. Tremors became an intermezzo in our daily lives inside the soccer stadium. The regular trembles of the ground beneath our feet did not stop us from carrying out our activities. We got used to them. But one day, in the afternoon, the structure of the stadium suddenly started letting out rumbling noises. The ground wobbled, the tent poles squeaked, the tents tottered and we could not stand firmly. For a few seconds, which seemed like forever, the universe felt deeply quiet. Then all at once the air was filled with screams and wailing.

I was trembling, but made myself look calm and started calling the people to gather in the middle of the soccer field. Many dwellers ran to join me in the camp's safety point, but some only wept and stayed in their tents as if they were pinned there. The daily workers and security guards ran into the tents and guided those who stayed inside the tents to come out and join us. Outside the stadium, we could hear the muffled rumble of motorbikes and car engines, and the panicked mob screaming, "tsunami…tsunami is coming". All of us inside the camp were scared to death as well, and wanted to run somewhere for refuge before the seawater reached us. But instead, we remained huddled up in the middle of the camp as if there was a power that held us together. We wanted to face whatever lay ahead of us together with the people we lived with in the camp.

The tsunami never came that day. Even after it was safe, though, we continued staying in the safety point for some moments and pondering the natural act that had just threatened our lives. Regardless of our ethnic group, sex, age, religion or position, we shared the same fear of the brutality of armed conflict and the destructive potential of natural forces. What else could have better convinced us that we were all the same creature trying to survive on the surface of mother earth?

Now, even years after that experience in Banda Aceh, the kinship that grew in the camp still warms my heart. I still feel a lifetime bond of friendship offered by the same people who once greeted me with hatred when our life paths first crossed.

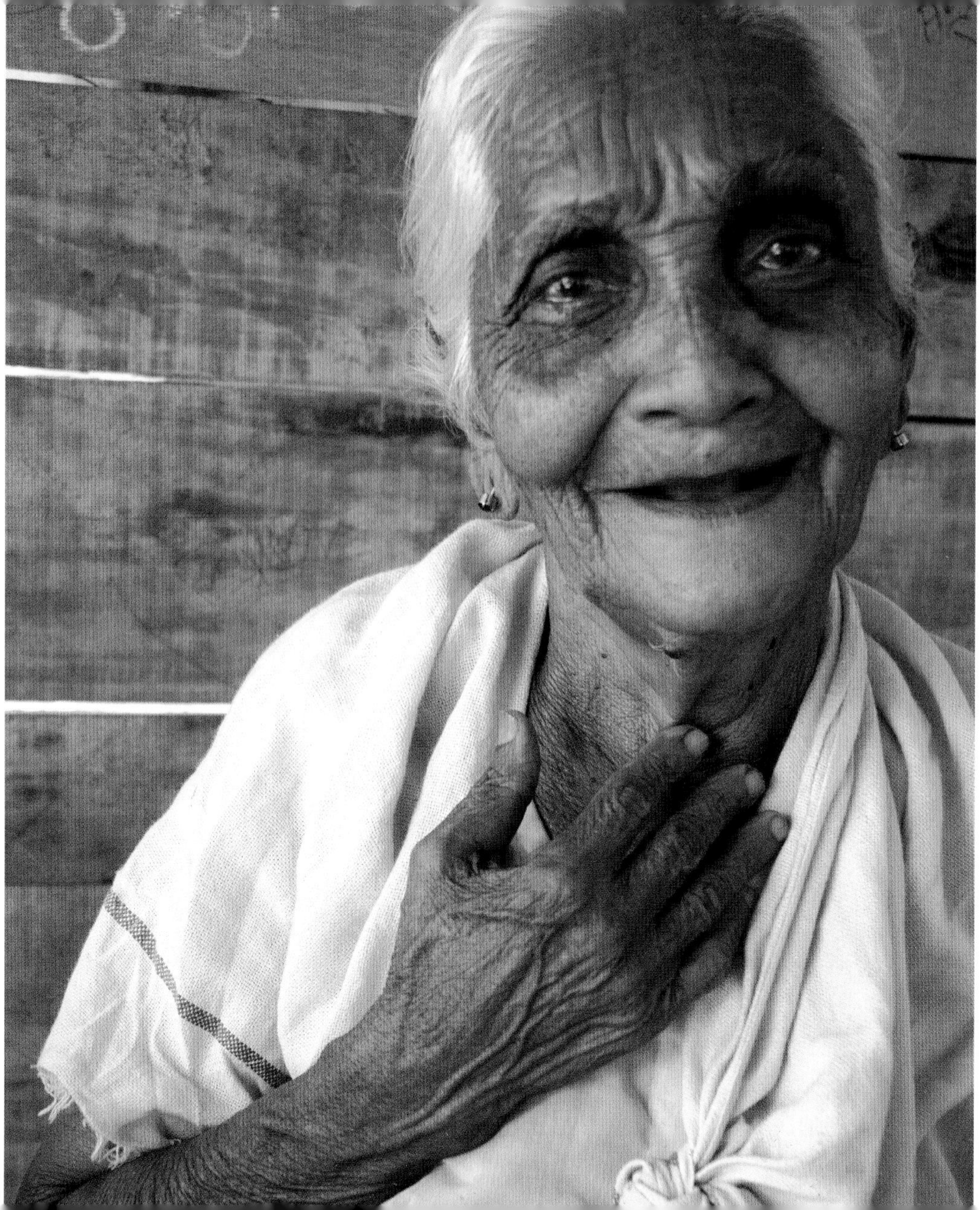

JILL SCHNOEBELEN • USA

Embrace

I tugged at my headscarf and tried the phone number again. It should have been simple enough—placing a call home to the US to say I'd arrived safely to the International Islamic University of Malaysia's campus. I was jetlagged, unaccustomed to the humidity, hungry but unable to eat, and felt like I was in over my (covered) head. I was to be a visiting student for the next year as part of a Fulbright Fellowship. I had anticipated that wearing the required headscarf would be an enlightening experiment, perhaps taking a bit of getting used to, but something I could handle. That first night, though, I panicked. Even the woman outlined on the bathroom door sign was wearing a headscarf.

After excusing myself from my gender-segregated table at the welcome reception, I spent two hours unsuccessfully trying to get a payphone anywhere on campus to work. Just when I had given up hope and returned, defeated, to the girls' dormitory, I came upon another student who had just finished her call and she offered me her assistance and calling card. As soon as I heard my mother's voice, I felt like crying out of relief.

When I hung up the phone, I surprised myself by asking this stranger for a hug. Reflecting on it, I suppose I needed physical reassurance that everything really was going to be alright and that I wasn't as alone as I felt. Shukriah—the root of her name is Arabic for 'thanks'—was perhaps a bit bewildered, but nevertheless obliged and invited me to tea the next day.

When I arrived at her room, I was greeted by Islam's multicultural faces: Indian-Mauritian Shukriah, Tanzanian Farida, Chinese-Malaysian Buddhist convert Hidaya, Kenyan Rahma, and Indonesian Nurah. For the next few days, I found myself talking with them about our lives, families, studies and, on occasion, Islam. They knew I was non-Muslim—without religion really—but welcomed my questions and asked their own. They never tried to convert, only to educate. Accompanying our conversations was spicy East African tea. Farida, a Food Science Ph.D. student,

A woman gestures to her heart during a moment of connection shared with the photographer in a relief camp in Kerala, India, after the 2004 Asian Tsunami. photo by jennifer esperanza

produced meals with only a rice cooker and some culinary magic. As Islam stipulates, I was treated as a guest my first three days with them. What truly moved me, however, was that they immediately embraced me as a friend.

After many days spent together in the girls' dormitory, we readied ourselves to go to a campus restaurant. I pulled on the headscarf Farida had given me and that I came to favor—a big, black veil with lace at the bottom where it hit my waist, already sewn together so there was no trouble with pins. They put on their own scarves and long, black robes. It wasn't until that moment that I discovered that Shukriah and Rahma were niqabettes—women who wear the full veil, with only their eyes peering out.

I instantly recognized my good fortune: I had gotten to know these women before my stereotypes could come into play and prevent me from interacting normally with them. If I had first met them fully veiled, I would have been intimidated. I never would have approached them on the street in full cover, naively anticipating some kind of vow of silence on their part. Their face veils would have been the defining feature and it would have been hard for me to get past my own assumptions: conservative women who never would want to be friends with an infidel. My own close-mindedness would have kept me from the lively conversations and easy friendships I stumbled upon.

A group of Muslim and Hindu school friends travel together on a ferry outside of Trincomalle, along the eastern coast of Sri Lanka. Elsewhere in the region tensions have erupted between Muslim and Hindus, sometimes resulting in violent conflict.
photo by michal przedlacki

The phantoms I had seen floating around campus suddenly had bodies and feet, faces and voices. These are independent, opinionated, and smart women. In the company of women, their vibrancy filled whatever room they were in till it was bursting and energized me. Their vivid personalities, however, were tempered by modesty and moral conviction once they entered the wider world.

I learned to recognize my friends from purses, posture, shoes and eyes from meters away. Rahma's black gown somehow always gave me the impression that she was taller than she really was. Quickly, the fact that they wore niqab faded into the background.

After a few months, Rahma let it slip that Shukriah had told them about our first encounter—my request for a hug—and they had all been amused by it. From that time on, they'd tease me with an offer of a hug each time we met. I self-censored the boy drama I normally share with friends, but remember animated conversations. Our purpose on earth: Shukriah claimed it is to worship God; I argued that didn't make sense because it would

mean a selfish God. I still haven't figured out how Islam reconciles free will with pre-destination despite their attempts to explain it. Day-to-day life and future plans: Rahma hopes for a dozen children and that she will be her future husband's first wife, but that there will be others. She is from a large, polygamous family and wants the same. Culture: they wanted to know, just what do those Americans carry around in their big backpacks all the time?

My college roommate—an American training to be a Buddhist nun in a South Korean temple—came to visit and I knew these women who shared so much in conviction and faith, though different religions, had to meet. It was Amanda's first time talking to conservative Muslim women and their first time talking to a Buddhist nun-in-training. As they lined up to pray, we sat back and watched. Rahma led the Muslim sisters in prayer; thinking of it now, I wish I could hear those beautiful, melodic words again. When they finished, they asked Amanda to demonstrate how she prays—bowing has a prominent role within both forms of worship—and joked if I had a special way of not praying. I marvel even now at all the openness, understanding and curiosity that filled the room.

I left Malaysia in the middle of Ramadan. For our last meal together, we took over Rahma's room as usual and Farida cooked up dish after delicious dish. Nurah accompanied Hidaya to the store to pick up last minute ingredients. Since I was not fasting that day, I was the taste-tester, advising on more salt, more sugar. As the call to prayer sounded, we ate dates, the same way the Prophet broke fast. To me it felt like Thanksgiving—how happy I was that I had asked a stranger for a hug.

64

The joyful dance of two friends on an early spring morning is framed by the cobbled streets of Guildford, England, and the city beyond.
photo by andy teo

CHAPTER 5

Celebrating Life

Sudiksha's Zen Piddle

Sudiksha, an eternally curious three-year-old, and I, a slightly-bored-slightly-forty-year-old, were traveling together to Ranikhet recently with other family members. As soon as the vehicle was on the highway she turned to me, "Tauji, when will we reach Ranikhet?"

"Oh, it's a long way off. It will take us seven or eight hours to get there," I said.

After about half an hour she wanted to know if we were within striking distance. I told her it was still a long way off. She asked the same question after twenty minutes.

"We'll get there when it's dark," I said.

"Oh, that's a long way off," she said.

When we reached Haldwani, she was tremendously excited at seeing the hills.

"Will there be snow?" she wanted to know.

"If we're lucky..." I said, and then to get her in the mood, I inhaled deeply and said, "Hmmm, I'm liking the air!"

Two children, among the many who sell trinkets at various temples at Siem Riep in Cambodia, welcome a moment of play outside the temple. photo by azli jamil

As we climbed the hills, she started inhaling deeply and saying, "Tauji, I'm liking the air!"

"That's nice. How much are you liking it?"

She thought for a moment and said, "More than twenty."

"When will the road stop going round and round?" she wanted to know next.

"When we have reached Ranikhet."

"Tauji, now we are going down!"

"That's because we have to cross a hill before we reach Ranikhet."

"How many hills do we have to cross?"

"Three more," I guessed.

"Hmmm...I'm liking it!"

We arrived when it was dark. The next morning those of us that managed to get up early went out for a short trek. Sudiksha was with us. After walking for a kilometer or so she came up to me and said, "Tauji, I'm tired now."

"Shall we turn back?" I asked.

"No, I was thinking I could sit on your lap," she said.

I hoisted her on my wheelchair and she sat astride my lap. She inhaled deeply and said, "Hmmm...I'm liking it!"

We were walking through a cantonment and the trees had various signs on them. I read them out aloud in a singsong way to entertain her.

"Is this a new song?" Sudiksha asked me as I read out, "Ped dharaa ka abhushan hai, karta dur pradushan hai." *[Trees are earth's ornaments, they get rid of pollution]*

"Yes," I said hoping she'd join in.

"It's a funny song. Stop singing it."

Then I found a nice one and started singing again, "Dharti ki yahi pukaar, Vriksha se karo mera uddhaar." *[The earth has just one call; my uplifting is through trees]*

"Has the earth caught a cold?" Sudiksha inquired.

"Why?"

"Then why does it want us to apply Vicks?" *[The Hindi for trees, 'Vriksha', sounds a lot like Vicks.]*

Later, in the afternoon we drove to Machkali, offering gorgeous views of the snow-clad Himalayan ranges. Even though it was about three o'clock, we could see the full moon rising from behind the Himalayas. Sudiksha wanted to know the flavor of the snow on the mountains. Then, answering her own question, she said, "looks like vanilla." I had not thought of Nanda Devi, Trishul, Nand Kot and the Pindari glacier as being vanilla flavored and the thought was delicious.

A grandfather sits with his grandson outside of his schoolhouse in Lhasa, Tibet. photo by hendro hioe

As we stood taking in the beauty, Sudiksha piped in, "Mujhe rabbits ke paas jaa kar susu karni hai!" *[I want to piddle next to rabbits.]*

I almost fell off my wheelchair. I felt like I had been touched by a Zen master. Here we were, standing in a loud silence, admiring the overpowering beauty of the mountains and Sudiksha's mind was thinking of peeing among rabbits. In a flash I could see that with all my education and professional pre-occupations, I had lost track of the real meaning of life.

Ever since we've returned from Ranikhet I've been telling my wife that I also feel like peeing next to rabbits.

NATALI ROJAS • COLOMBIA

Through My Camera

I woke up this morning to a rainy day in Bogotá, Colombia. Still, I run towards my window as I do each morning, trying to catch the first sunlight. Since I've come home, I start my days enjoying the mountains and light that surround me. I love when I feel the earth breathing and its fresh air touching my skin. I am alive.

I begin each day with a cup of coffee and some "arepas" (Columbian corn bread) in my hand. The smell of arepas transports me to my childhood: those breakfasts at my grandparents' house and the games that we once played together. With my eyes closed I hold the photograph that I found this morning in the living room: José, my grandfather, is wearing his favorite blue sweater. The stick in his right hand matches the wooden frame of the portrait. I can still hear his breath and feel the warmth that I captured through my camera ten years ago.

Abuelo (grandfather): I wish you were here today so I could share with you my vision of the world. My life is like an artwork made up of many different shades, tones, colors, shapes… images. Every day your smile, strength, and wise advice, along with the people, places, climates, landscapes, dreams and life experiences I have had, inspire this composition. I know my return home to Columbia would be a joy for you as it has been for my grandmother and parents. I wish we could share these feelings with you, dear *abuelo*.

I have only spent three months back home; enough time to discover how sensitive I am to everything that surrounds me. Smells, places, sounds… and memories that I thought were lost have been aroused and are deeply connecting me to life. I have come to Colombia with the purpose of working towards peace through the use of arts. I have joined a team of community youth leaders in Ciudad Bolivar, a low income district located in southern Bogotá. Ciudad Bolivar has been a historical meeting point for displaced people from all corners of Colombia, and has for many years been considered one of the most dangerous areas of the Colombian capital. But where there is darkness, there is also light. Here we are teaching children how to use cameras to explore their

fears, emotions and dreams and communicate with the world.

Bogotá is really different from the other places where I have lived for the past seven years. However, everywhere humans eat and sing, dream and hope, we all fall in love… Why not share those experiences with others? What do we fear? In Ciudad Bolivar, where the art project I work with runs, children are using photography and films to reflect and question who they are. Through alternative and creative channels they are raising questions and open dialogues with their families, friends and the world that surrounds them. Children do not fear. They have so much to teach.

Grandfather: I had no fears when I decided to move abroad and study. I was curious about the appearance of the sky, the smell of the air and the way people talked in other parts of the world. And I had the chance to travel and share with others. I learned and I grew. I still am growing! You know that my dreams´ limits have always been skies. Your portrait, the children's pictures and videos, and the ones I have taken through these years enrich my existence. Those images make my life brighter and fill it with colors.

Abuelo: Every time my finger presses the shutter I feel as if the world has stopped for a moment. I listen quietly, and I observe in detail the light, how the spirit of things looks.
I usually forget about time and place, I lose my fears.

Through my camera,
dancing with the richness of life
finding light in unexpected places
for a moment
I come to life.

Eleven year old Goodson Nyirenda captures a moment of laughter among his friends at a youth centre located in the slums of Lusaka, Zambia.
photo by goodson nyirenda

KUSUMITA PEDERSEN • USA

On Gorham Mountain

A fire swept over Mount Desert Island
When I was one year old.
For eleven days it flamed and spread.
Where mountains come down to the sea
Their pine forests were burned away.
Westward they were left green.

When I was a child we would walk
On burned mountains with no woods,
The pink granite blackened and bare,
The trees charred stumps, around us
Low bushes, hot sun and open space,
The ocean stretching below.

We would cross a line to mountains
That had not been burned
And walk deep in pine woods
Dim, mossy and fragrant
By lakes and cool streams,
Seeing the ocean from the summit.

My father said the woods
On our burned mountains
Would be all grown back
When I had become old.
He is gone. That time is close.
O mountain where we used to walk,
I have come back to find you.

My mountain, you are green again.
Your path goes through spruce trees
Higher than the birch and aspen
Who grew first after the fire.
Only a searching eye can see
Soot-darkened stone and
Burned wood of hidden trunks.
Only from your high ridge
Can I see the ocean now.

New life sprouts out of an old tree in Dhanmondi Lake, Dhaka, Bangladesh.
photo by ahmed sharif

The pines are still to come.
When they have grown tall
And your forests are dense,
I will be gone – like a tree
Consumed into air by fire.
But you, my mountain,
Will be in me still
Wherever I will live
And I will be here ever,
Still in you by the sea,
Burned and grown again.

Mount Desert Island is on the Atlantic Ocean on the coast of Maine, the farthest northeast of the United States. The feeling of inseparable oneness that I have had with the island's mountains, woods and waters since my earliest childhood has formed me for my entire life. What is unexpected about this sense of connection is that as the years pass, the depth, power and central importance of this experience only continue to grow and grow.

Afterword BY LEONARDO BOFF

Hope That is Born from a New Delivery of Mother Earth

Throughout the planet we can perceive the awakening of a new consciousness, and the urgency of creating a sense of common destiny and belonging of all with one another and with Mother Earth.

A number of social movements such as the Arab Spring and "Occupiers" have recently emerged as a sign of this new state of consciousness. These social movements have started a new kind of revolution; the revolution of horizontality. Social media and cell phones have created connections among and between us, from the city to the countryside. Suddenly a collective feeling of creative and transformative connection has been formed.

Many of the multitudes arising now do not report to the classic flags of the left, or even to the dreams expressed as part of the World Social Forum for another possible world. Many claim, in a very original way, the minimum necessary for the 'good life': social justice with ecological justice; participative democracy; human rights; women's equal presence; jobs; the transparency of public authorities. Many mobilize a forceful critique of an economic system that sacrifices entire communities to meet the greed of banks, and many especially reject a market in which everything is set as merchandise, including the most vital and irreplaceable assets—water, seeds, food. Many speak out against the irrefutable devastation of our natural world.

Dandelion seeds fly like parachutes against the blue sky of late summer in Tuusula, southern Finland. photo by tomi nytorp

From this vigorous social energy, carried forth especially by youth, a new set of ideas is being born. These ideas will create the conditions for a different way of living on this planet, and discovering ourselves as a human species, reunited with the community of life.

We are walking towards meeting the dream of Pierre Teilhard de Chardin, who anticipated in the increasing connections among peoples, the advent of a new phase in the history of humanity and the Earth. He called this noosphere, or the increased interaction and integration of minds and hearts united in the same human dwelling. It will be "the new beginning" called for in the Earth Charter; a beginning that requires "a change of mind and heart... a new sense of global interdependence and universal responsibility".

The pain that we are suffering is not from a dying person in the nausea of death, but of a delivery that will give birth to a new life. This life has already begun as demonstrated by the many seminal examples in this book. Through each moment of connection, with each other, with ourselves, with the Earth, we are moving in the direction of a more eco-friendly and bio-centered civilization. This will put life in its immense diversity in the center, human life and the life of the living Earth.

Let us not underestimate the transformative power that a single moment of connection can have. Let us not stop walking forward together until all human beings feel part of the great Whole, citizens, brothers and sisters, living with one another at home.

Editors

Lisa Marika Jokivirta, Finland/Canada is a social scientist, educator and sustainability activist who deeply believes in the transformative power of storytelling and the arts. She has most recently enjoyed working as Junior Lecturer in the Master's Program in Development and International Cooperation at the University of Jyväskylä, Finland, and is currently undertaking her PhD fieldwork in northernmost Lapland as part of a four year post funded by the Academy of Finland. Alongside her research, Lisa is also a writer, violin player, a bit of a nomad by nature, and a great admirer of communal life.

Anna Duhon, USA lives in rural New York, where she does social and cultural research on the interconnections between people, nature, and agriculture, as part of the Hawthorne Valley Farmscape Ecology Program. She completed a BA in Social Anthropology from Harvard University, and a Master of Arts in Natural Resources and Peace from the UN-mandated University for Peace in Costa Rica. Anna is deeply interested in processes of personal and global transformation, and grateful for all of the 'moments' that have helped show the way.

Shannon Walsh, Canada was born and raised on Vancouver Island on the west coast of Canada, where she has spent the past several years as a secondary school teacher. Currently, she is working on her Master's Degree in Development and International Cooperation in Finland. Despite her Canadian roots, Shannon can feel at home almost anywhere, with a particular love for Zambia and India. Her part in this book comes from a deep belief that we are all connected and that the realization of that leads to compassion, courage, and kindness.

Authors

A. James Wohlpart, USA is Interim Dean of Undergraduate Studies at Florida Gulf Coast University. He is a Professor of English, with a specialty in Environmental Literature, and a Senior Scholar with the Center for Environmental and Sustainability Education. He has published two co-edited books, as well as over twenty articles in journals and collections on ecopedagogy, sustainability, environmental literature, nineteenth-century American literature and creative nonfiction essays on sense of place.

Aditi Rao, India is a writer, educator, and activist. She currently resides in New Delhi, where she works as a consultant for non-profit organizations in the field of peace education and youth development. She also facilitates creative writing workshops at educational institutions, and carves out time for her twin passions of poetry and pottery. She holds a Master of Fine Arts in Creative Writing from Sarah Lawrence College (New York) and a Bachelor of Liberal Art from Soka University of America.

Blair Braverman, USA graduated from Colby College in 2011 with a degree in environmental policy, and is now a Master of Fine Arts candidate at the University of Iowa's Nonfiction Writing Program. She has worked as a dogsled guide, naturalist, and cartographer in Norway and the United States. She has also worked and written for multiple NGOs on issues of environmental health and justice, and was heavily involved in efforts to pass safer chemicals legislation in the state of Maine.

David Suzuki, Canada/Japan is an acclaimed geneticist and environmentalist and the co-founder of the David Suzuki

Foundation. He is the author of more than forty books and is the recipient of the 2009 Right Livelihood Award, the UNSECO Kalinga Prize for Science, the United Nations Environmental Medal, and the UNEP's Global 500 award, and he has been named a Companion of the Order of Canada. In addition, he has been adopted into three First Nations clans. He lives in Vancouver, British Columbia.

Elina Helander-Renvall, Sápmi (Finland) was born and lives in Utsjoki, Northern Finland. She is a renowned author and artist. She works at the University of Lapland's Arctic Center as a senior scientist, and is the director of the Arctic Indigenous Peoples and Sami Research Office. In addition to her research on the Sami language and culture, she has investigated biological diversity, reindeer herding, Indigenous knowledge, and customary law among the Indigenous peoples of the Arctic. Prior to the Arctic Centre, she worked as director for the Nordic Sami Institute in Kautokeino, Norway.

Emma Milliken, Anishnaabe Nation of Canada is an Aboriginal Nations educator at Spectrum Community School in Victoria, British Columbia, Canada. She supports high school students with First Nations, Metis, and Inuit ancestry. Emma is continually inspired by her students, and one of her greatest joys is watching her students graduate and continue their journeys to post secondary education, careers and jobs. She reads, writes and draws as often as she can, and has recently been trying to improve her halting Ojibway.

Husnur Esthiwahyu, Indonesia (Esthi) is a humanitarian worker from Indonesia. She has worked in various humanitarian operations and emergency responses in Indonesia, as well as during recovery and reconstruction phases in collaboration with different international organizations. Working in natural disaster situations and armed conflict torn areas makes her appreciate humanity more. Esthi is very interested in humanitarian assistance, disaster risk reduction, and food security issues. She also loves reading and traveling.

Jill Schnoebelen, USA holds a B.A. in Political Science from Yale University and a Master of Arts in International Law and Human Rights from the University for Peace (Costa Rica). After living in Malaysia, Egypt, Ghana, Yemen, and Costa Rica, Jill found her way back home to Iowa in 2009. She is focused on making a difference in the community where she was raised as the Volunteer Center and Community Impact Coordinator at the United Way of Johnson County and through her own volunteer efforts. Jill enjoys exploring and experimenting in the kitchen, garden and, most recently, woodshop.

Kusumita Pedersen, USA is Professor of Religious Studies at St. Francis College in Brooklyn, New York. She received her doctorate in Buddhist Studies from Columbia University and was previously Executive Director of the Project on Religion and Human Rights and Executive Director of the Temple of Understanding. Deeply involved in the interfaith movement for more than twenty-five years, she is Co-Chair of the Interfaith Center of New York and active with the Council for a Parliament of the World's Religions.

Leonardo Boff, Brazil is one of the founders of liberation theology, and a theologian, philosopher and writer known for his active support for the rights of the poor and excluded. In 1984, the Congregation for the Doctrine of the Faith in Rome silenced him for a year for his book 'Church: Charisma and Power'. Later he became a Professor of Ethics and Philosophy of Religion at the State University of Rio de Janeiro. He

is the author of more than 100 books, and continues to speak at conferences on spirituality, ecology, ethics, and ecumenical theology in Brazil and abroad. He is a member of the Earth Charter Commission.

Mary Evelyn Tucker, USA is co-director of the Forum on Religion and Ecology at Yale University where she is a senior lecturer and research scholar at the School of Forestry and Environmental Studies and the Divinity School. Along with Brian Swimme she has created Journey of the Universe, which is a book, film, and educational series. She has been involved with the Earth Charter since its inception. She was a member of the Earth Charter drafting committee from 1997-2000 and has served on the Earth Charter International Council since 2000.

Michael J. Cohen, USA is a Program Director of the Institute of Global Education where he coordinates its Integrated Ecology Department and Project NatureConnect. He also serves on the Ecopsychology faculty of Portland State University and the Akamai University Institute of Applied Ecopsychology whose program he initiated and has directed since 1990. Dr. Cohen is also an accomplished folk song artist and contra dancer who presents traditional music using three instruments.

Natali Rojas, Colombia grew up in Bogota, Colombia. At 18, she left home and has been roaming the world ever since. She studied Sociology and Art History in Spain, and is currently finishing a MA in Development and International Cooperation at the University of Jyväskylä, Finland. In 2010, her love for her homeland and passion for community arts took her back to Ciudad Bolivar in Colombia, the subject of her story in this book. Natali currently lives in a remote village in New Zealand… she keeps taking pictures of mountains, sunsets, people and the colors that brighten her life.

Rabbi Awraham Soetendorp, The Netherlands is an award-winning lecturer, writer, environmental activist and champion of civil society. He is a founding member of Green Cross International, and the Islam and the West Dialogue Group of the World Economic Forum. He serves as an Earth Charter Commissioner, and is the founder and president of the Jacob Soetendorp Institute for Human Values that helps to build bridges between the cultures, spiritual traditions, and generations. He and his wife Sira are blessed with two daughters and six grandchildren.

Salil Chaturvedi, India lives with his wife in Goa, India. In December 2009 he, along with a crew of three, sailed a twenty-foot sloop from Mumbai to Goa to draw attention to accessibility issues for disabled persons. Salil himself was partially paralyzed in an accident in 1984 and uses a wheelchair. Currently, Salil spends his time planning his forest garden that he hopes to set up in Goa, and is passionate about leading a low-energy, sustainable lifestyle, writing poetry, and following Taoist principles that he believes will bring healing to the Earth and its communities.

Wangari Maathai, Kenya is internationally recognized for her persistent struggle for democracy, human rights, and environmental conservation. She developed the idea of planting trees into a broad-based, grassroots organization called the Green Belt Movement, which was launched in 1977 and is responsible for the planting of more than thirty million trees across Kenya. In 2004, she was awarded the Nobel Peace Prize. Wangari Maathai was also an Earth Charter Commissioner and spokesperson. She passed away in 2011, and this book is dedicated in memory of her life, work and spirit, which continue to inspire people around the world.

Photographers

Aaron Lutsch, Canada is a teacher and photographer. He has an ardent desire to capture the quality and essence of creativity in his work, while sharing his passion with his students. *www.rwophotography.com*

Ahmed Sharif, Bangladesh is a self-taught photographer. Though he has a full-time job outside of photography, he finds time to travel, take photos, and mentor young photographers.

Andy Teo, UK is a family physician and photographer from the UK. He is also a keen jazz pianist and occasional guitar strummer. *http://www.photocillin.co.uk/*

Anas Bukhash, United Arab Emirates is an amateur photographer originally from Dubai and educated in the USA. He has a passion for football.

Anna Jokivirta, Finland/ Canada recently moved from Canada to Finland. She is studying to become a nurse and has a strong interest in cross-cultural care.

Ashish Tibrewal, India was born in India, but now lives in the USA. He enjoys practicing photography with his favorite subjects, his young family.

Azli Jamil, Malaysia was educated in the USA in the field of Information Systems. He left the corporate sector to pursue his photography and writing career. *www.wix.com/azlijamil/azlijamilphotography/*

Ben Visbeek, The Netherlands lives in the Netherlands with his wife and two kids. He started taking photos at the age of 8, during his first school trip to the zoo.

Clayton Scott, Australia was born in New Zealand and is a proud Maori. He regularly attends cultural events and shares his photos to raise awareness of indigenous cultures.

Corrado Giulietti, Italy is an editor for an information and media company. He is also a blogger, photographer, and journalist. *http://www.flickr.com/photos/corradogiulietti/*

Dave Brosha, Canada is a personal, adventure, and landscape photographer living in Northern Canada with his young family. *www.davebrosha.com*

David Stephenson, Ireland is a photographer who was born in Dublin, and publishes his work in many national and international newspapers and art journals. *http://davidstephenson.ie/*

Edward Butterworth, England/Canada lives in Victoria, British Columbia. He teaches communication skills and leads personal growth workshops.

Fabio Moscatelli, Italy lives in Rome, where he is a professional sound engineer with a passion for photography.

Fahim Hossain, Bangladesh is studying urban and regional planning at the Bangladesh University of Engineering and Technology. *http://www.flickr.com/photos/fahim_123752/*

Goodson Nyirenda, Zambia age 13, lives in Garden Compound in Lusaka, Zambia. He is an active member of the YOFOSO Youth Centre.

Hans Hendriksen, The Netherlands started his own travel photography business in 2007 after shooting his travel highlights for 17 years. *www.hanshendriksen.net*

Hendro Hioe, Indonesia is a chief operating officer for a furniture manufacturing company and the head of a printing company in Jakarta, Indonesia.

Izla Kaya Bardavid, Sweden is a public health professional doing humanitarian and development work with an international NGO called ADRA. She was born in Sweden, with proud Assyrian roots.

Jennifer Esperanza, USA is a fine art, portrait, editorial and social justice photographer. She lives in Santa Fe, New Mexico and is the mother of two. *www.jenniferesperanza.com*

Juan Carlos Pina, Mexico is an ecologist and photographer with a passion for photography, video recordings of natural landscapes, rock climbing and mountaineering. *www.bioxplora.com.mx*

Karsten Lehmkuhl, Germany works for FedEx alongside raising his young family.

Luca Gargano, Italy is a wine merchant in Italy. He is currently preparing a book of pictures he took in remote villages in Africa.

Lucia Paprčková, Slovakia studied Comparative Literature in Prague. She has worked as a freelance photographer and translator.

Marcelo Eduardo Salgado, Brazil is a graduate in economics. He has a special interest in photographing the people and nature of his native Brazil. *http://www.panoramio.com/user/7562*

Maria Josephine Wijiastuti, Indonesia enjoys exploring life's moments and nature's beauty through photography, and has experience working in humanitarian efforts.

Michal Przedlacki, Poland is a humanitarian aid worker, published author, and photographer. *www.flickr.com/photos/dziadek.*

Mina Jokivirta, Finland is a graphic designer who loves being in and around nature. Her small rural community is what matters to her most.

Mohamed Sifah Saeed, Maldives is interested in capturing nature, portraits, art, and everyday life in his country.

Mohammad Rakibul Hasan, Bangladesh is a photojournalist from Dhaka, Bangladesh. His photography can be seen at: *www.falconphotoagency.com*

Naomi Frerotte, France is a passionate video advocate, photographer and development worker, currently carrying out research in post conflict Uganda.

Oluyemisi Joel-Osebor, Nigeria is a woman with a passion for international development. She is a Development Economist and Social Entrepreneur.

Pim Stouten, the Netherlands is based in Amsterdam and works for a multinational publishing company.

Samer Muscati, Canada is a lawyer, documentary photographer, and journalist.

Sundeep Bali, India is a lens-based artist. He has exhibited widely in India, the Netherlands, New Zealand and the US. *www.sundeepbali.com*

Thomas Hawk, USA has a love for the quirky and absurd side of photography. *http://thomashawk.com/*

Thomas Suryono, Indonesia is a geologist surveyor from Indonesia. He also likes to work as a freelance photographer focusing on stories of human life.

Tomi Nytorp, Finland works as a carpenter and woodworker at his own woodwork shop in southern Finland. He's an active climber and nature lover. *http://www.tominytorp.com/*

Tri Silvanto, Indonesia has worked on humanitarian issues for the last ten years. He firmly believes that a single photo can change the world.

Ville Miettinen, Finland is a serial entrepreneur and world traveler who picked up photography as a hobby six years ago in order to document his travels.

First Endpaper Collage (from top left to right): *La'iqaah and Ashura* by Lucia Paprovic, *One Usipa* by Izla Kaya Bardavid, *Harvest* by David Stephenson, *Milk* by Fabio Moscatelli, *Elephant Walk* by Lisa Jokivirta, *Baby's Bath* by Naomi Frerotte, *Tibetan Child Monks, Practicing Football* by Samer Muscati, *Himalayan moon* by Salil Chaturyedi, *Wordless Welcome* by Anna Jokivirta, *Lost in the Music* by Cor rado Giulietti, *Peek* by Maria Josephine *Wijiastuti*, *Father and Son* by Ashish Tibrewal, *Coffee Community* by David Stephenson, *Always Together* by Luca Gargano.

Last Endpaper Collage: *Rice Fields and Prayer Flags* by Sundeep Bali, *Compassion* by Anas Bukhash, *Blessing* by Ashish Tibrewal, *Happy to See You* by Corrado Giulietti, *Familglia* by Corrado Giulietti, *Friends* by Corrado Giulietti, *Balance* by Aaron Lutsch, *Busy in the Backyard* by Tomi Nytorp, *Introduction* by Karsten Lehmkuhl, *Mimi the Legend* by Hendro Hioe, *Daybreak* by Marcelo Eduardo Salgado, *Forever Love* by Luca Gargano, *Art of the Maldives* by Mohamed Sifah Saeed, *Run, Run, Run* by Ahmed Sharif, *Ashura on the Grass* by Lucia Paprovic, *Daily Throw* by Luca Gargano.

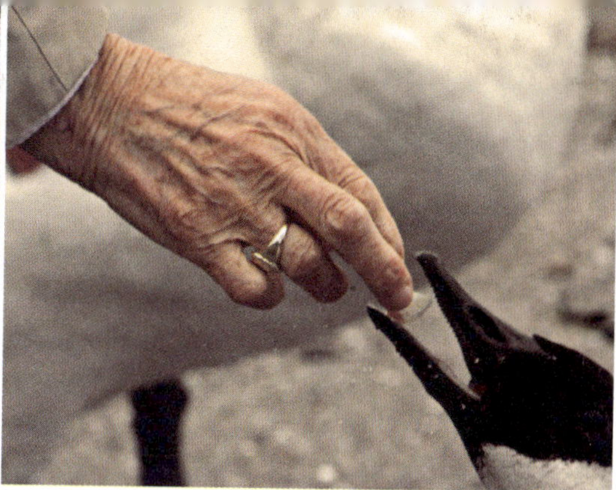